Dedications and Acknowledgments

To my children, Mirembe and Ttendo, that they find joy in learning to read.

To Dr. Festo Lugolobi, for his friendship, encouragement and support.

To Professor Dr. Rothfuss whose work inspired me.

To Lilo Klug, Summer Freemann, Christel Banghardt-Joest, Dorothy Kidza-Zentler,
am so honored to have you as special friends in my life.

Thanks to my family and friends for their love and support.

Special thanks to Ndawula family; Maria, Molly and Steve for the unending love and trust.

My deepest Gratitude to all that help to educate the poor
children and women of Uganda and around the World.

"This book is for the real Mirembe, who steals the show even if she is in the chorus."
Story though fictionalized, was suggested by a true story!!

Visit us on the web! www.africaculture.org

Some facts about Uganda

- Uganda is a landlocked country in eastern Africa. It is surrounded by Kenya to the east, Sudan to the north, Congo to the west, and Tanzania to the south.

- English is the most common language in the cities of Uganda, but there are around forty different languages that are regularly used in the country.

- Uganda has many delicious fruits including yummy pineapples, mangoes and bananas. They have a green banana that is called Matooke. It is one of the major foods there. It has a flavor similar to mashed potatoes.

- MIREMBE means peace and TTENDO means wonder in Luganda language.

- Peanuts are called ground nuts.

- In Uganda soccer is called football.

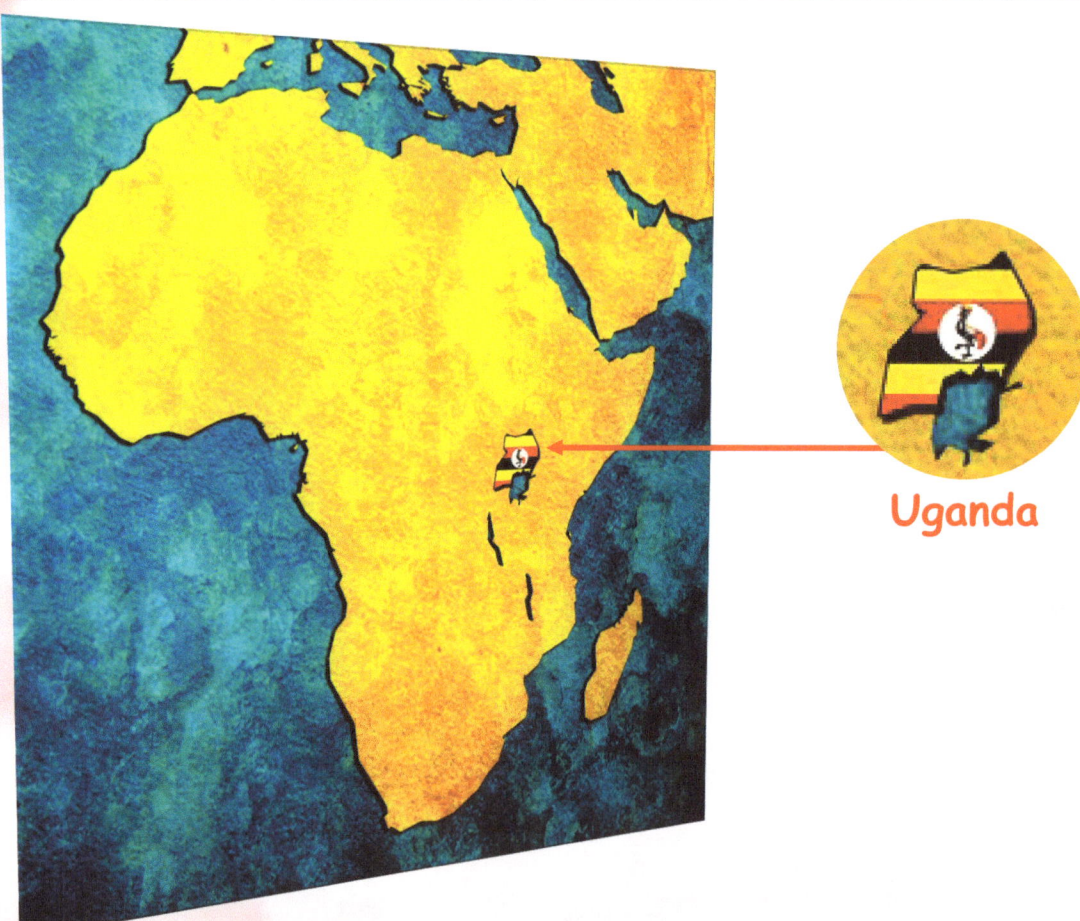

Uganda

Mirembe had always hoped that she would be able to visit Africa one day, she had no idea her dream was about to come true! For Summer break her Mother had a wonderful surprise..., they were all flying to Uganda! "

Hooray!!!", Mirembe exclaimed when she heard the news.
They would have to get up very early the next morning to get to the airport on time, because Africa is very far away.

Mirembe and her little brother Ttendo were so excited.
Mirembe thought the taxi could never drive fast enough!

Once at the airport, they saw many huge planes. They just couldn't wait to get inside a REAL airplane! Mirembe was thrilled that she was finally going to see where her mother had grown up. The place she had imagined in her mind many times. There were so many things that she wanted to see, but there were things that scared her too. She wondered……..

"Will I like it there…, will I be afraid of the darkness?". Mama said that lights go off so often. "Will I be able to climb trees, will I be able to carry baskets on top of my head like mama did when she was a child?". "Will I be able to play football……?" Mirembe's thoughts raced……..

After long security check-ups, they finally entered the airplane.
Wow! it was big! They were going to be on the plane for a long time;
luckily they had lots to do.
They watched TV, played games, read and slept.
Half way to Africa they had to get on a different plane.
After another long flight, Mirembe was finally in..........

UGANDA!!!!

They left the plane and entered the airport. Just as they went to pick their luggage, the airport went completely dark. All the lights had gone out! Mirembe was very scared! She looked up at her mother, "it's okay honey... electricity in Uganda is like a visitor, sometimes she is there and most times she is away". Mirembe laughed, mama always made her feel better.
Just then Ttendo pulled his flashlight! They used the tiny light to see while they picked up their bags and headed for the door.

Once outside they got into a big taxi bus that would take them to the village. As they drove, Mirembe noticed that the road was so narrow and bumpy. Mama explained that it was the big holes in the road that made the taxi bounce up and down all the way to the village.

As the taxi drove on, they couldn't believe their eyes......
there were cows and goats in the middle of the road! Mirembe
was surprised to see this narrow road being shared by everyone.
There were people walking and riding bicycles. Some of them carried
water on their heads, others tended to animals. Cars and motorcycles
were also using the road.

Ttendo had never seen animals like this before.
He could barely take his eyes off them.

"Mama, remember how you said I could get a pet when I turned six...,
can I have a cow please?" he asked excitedly.
His mama laughed and said she would think about it.

Finally they arrived at their Grandma and Grandpa's house. Everyone was so excited to finally meet for the very first time! Their grandparents lived in a real hut made of thatched grass and mud, just like mama had said. It felt cold and smooth.

When they entered the hut Mirembe got down on her knees to greet her Grandparents, just as her mother had taught her. Girls in Uganda do this to show respect for their elders. Young boys humble themselves by holding their hands together and bowing their head. Grandma was so happy to see that the children had learned the ways of Uganda! Mirembe felt proud to have made her Grandmother so happy.

Together they shared the fresh mango juice that Grandmother had prepared...Yummy in the tummy!

Soon it was time for bed; they were very tired from such a long trip. Mama, Mirembe and Ttendo all shared a mattress on the floor. It was very dark, but Mirembe felt safe next to her mother. She drifted off to sleep, her head filled with excitement for the days ahead.

The next morning Mirembe woke suddenly to the sound a very loud bird.... "Kokolilooooookoooo! Kokolilooooookoooo!" A rooster for an alarm clock..., how wonderful! Her thoughts raced as she wondered what their first day in the village would be like.

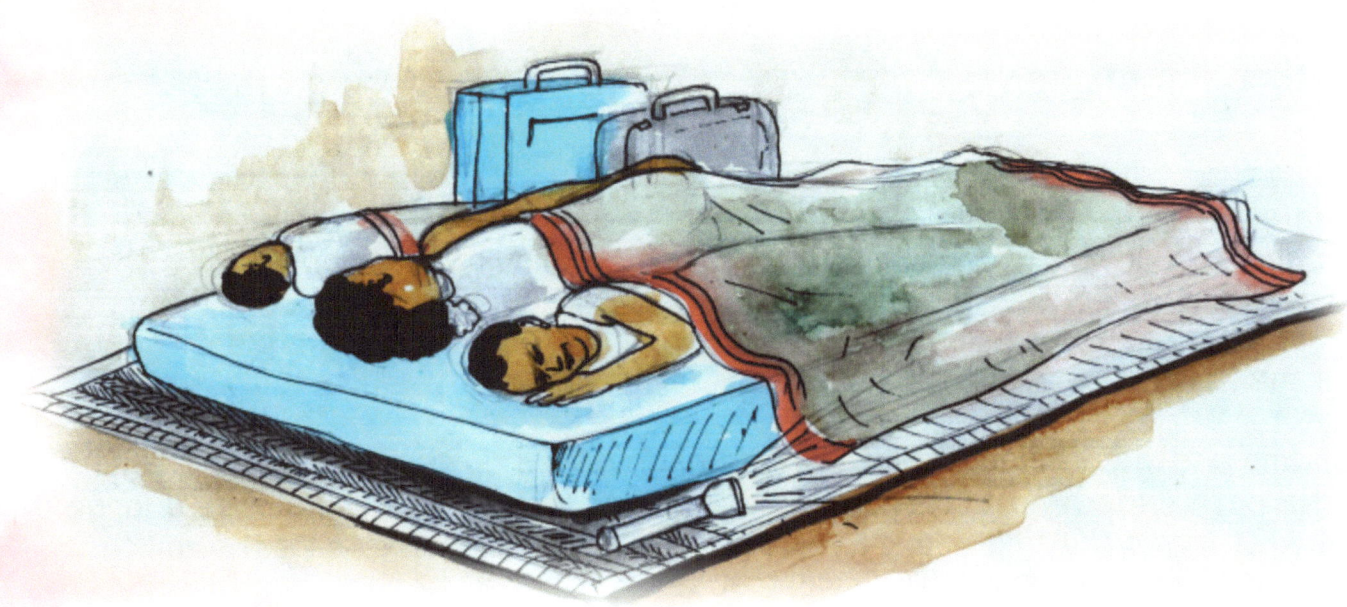

While getting dressed for the day, Mirembe could hear her tummy rumbling. Once her clothes were on she walked around a bit looking for the refrigerator...but she couldn't find it. "Grandma", she said "I'm so hungry, where do you keep your milk?" Her Grandmother giggled and smiled at her. "Let me show you", she said.

Grandma and the children went outside and walked down a small dirt path. As the path ended Mirembe could see Grandpa kneeling down next to a large animal. It was a COW!!!! Grandpa was milking a cow! "Where does the milk come out?" Ttendo asked. They were so excited...they both wanted to try! Grandfather taught them where to hold the cow, and told them they had to be very gentle. Both children took turns milking the cow. This was so exciting!

After milking the cow, Mirembe was quite dirty. Her Grandpa explained that there was no running water in their hut. They would have to go down to the well to fetch water for bathing, and cooking - just as they did every day. Mirembe followed Mama, and her cousin Maria down to the well. Maria explained that they must always be very careful as to not fall in. She watched with amazement as Maria got the water, it seemed a tricky.

When they got back to the hut, everyone was in the garden getting food and vegetables for dinner.

Mirembe wanted to dig too! Grandma taught her how to use the hoe, and Mama praised her for being such a wonderful gardener.

"Grandma, look how high I can climb!" yelled Ttendo as he hung from a tree branch.

Mirembe picked herself some beautiful flowers before they left for the hut.

As they walked home, Mirembe watched with amazement as Grandma and Mama balanced the food and firewood on their heads. They walked with such elegance…, she hoped she could learn to do that someday.

Ttendo happily pulled his new car behind him. He had made it from the bark of a banana tree, and banana fibers!

Mirembe was excited as the family all worked together to prepare dinner. There was no electricity in their hut, so they used three large rocks that they called "cooking stones". Mama added wood under and around the stones and lit a fire. They were making Matooke, a plantain that is boiled and mashed, and wrapped in a big banana leaf. It tastes very much like mashed potatoes, and it was Mirembe's favorite! They also made a peanut sauce. In Africa they call peanuts "ground nuts" because they grow underground.

After they all washed their hands, they sat down with the food in between them. When the children first saw their Grandparents eating with their fingers, Mirembe thought she should buy them some silverware with the money she had saved in her piggybank. After a while though, they mastered the art of eating with their fingers, and it became fun. Everyone in Uganda knows how to eat with their fingers.

The next morning they woke up early to go to church. Mirembe noticed that most of the women wore some special style of clothing, and also some of the men. Her Grandma explained that these were the traditional wear that people used for special occasions. The woman's outfits are called a "gomesi", and the men's clothing is called a "kanzu". Later that week Grandma came home with special gifts for Mirembe and Ttendo. The following Sunday they too put on their traditional wear. Mirembe felt just like a princess!

In the days that followed, Mirembe and Ttendo learned to do daily chores like all children of Uganda must do with their families. Since there was no running water to bathe, well water must be gotten every day. Firewood had to be gathered because they had no electricity to cook, or heat to their hut when it was cold. The garden had to be taken care of to ensure there were enough vegetables to eat.

Mirembe was relieved when her chores were finished and she could play with children who lived in the village.

Mirembe loved being in the village. After their chores, the children climbed trees and played "jumping sticks". They rolled down the hill and played hide and seek! There were so many places to run and hide. Not like back home where they mostly had to play inside the house.

There were even mango trees with tasty fruit to pick when they were hungry from playing. Yummy!!!

Mirembe and Ttendo had made so many new friends during their visit to Africa. Mirembe wanted to have a way to remember all of them, and she didn't want them to forget about her either. She had a brilliant idea..., friendship bracelets! She invited all her new friends to her Grandparent's hut and taught them how to make friendship bracelets. When they were finished they exchanged them with each other. With their new jewelry Mirembe was sure she would never forget this amazing trip, and all the friends she made!

Mirembe was enjoying every moment of her visit....every day she experienced something new. One day the boys in the village invited her to play ball with them. They were happy to see what a great player she was. It was so much fun!

Mirembe noticed that there weren't any shopping malls in the village..., in fact she couldn't remember seeing any stores at all! After talking with Mama, Mirembe decided that she wanted to give cousin Maria some of her clothes. People in Uganda had very few possessions compared to people in the United States where she lived. It made Mirembe feel good to share..., and her cousin Maria loved having the new clothing!

Mirembe had done so many wonderful things on her visit to Uganda. There was just one last thing that she really wanted to do. She wanted to see a real giraffe!

The whole family went to Murchison National Park, a sanctuary in Uganda that keeps wild animals safe from harm. They saw lots of elephants, hippopotamus, buffalos and giraffes! They even took a boat ride in the lake and saw beautiful birds resting along the shore. Everyone had an amazing time!

When they returned to the village that afternoon, Mirembe noticed two women who were doing a very interesting dance. Grandma explained that they were traditional experienced dancers. The ladies must have noticed Mirembe watching them because they walked over and invited her to join in the dance! They even dressed Mirembe in clothing just like their own. They all danced to African music called Baganda rhythm. Awesome!

That night would be Mirembe's last evening at her Grandparent's hut; she would be leaving the next day.

Grandma made a fire outside and they all sat around it while she told a story. Grandma loved to tell stories..., the endings changed depending on if the children were well behaved that day or not.

Mirembe listened to her Grandmother as she looked up into the African sky... she wanted this moment to last forever.

All too quickly it was morning. Their trip had ended way too soon!
She hugged her Grandma and held onto her tightly…, she hated to say
goodbye. "Thank you for the best holiday ever Grandma" said Mirembe
"I have learned so much! I cannot wait to come back again".

Grandma hugged Mama and Ttendo, and then they all got on the Boda Boda
(a bicycle taxi). Mirembe watched as the village got smaller and smaller as
they rode away. A piece of her would always live here in this tiny African
village. "Mama" she said "That was the best holiday ever".

THE END…..

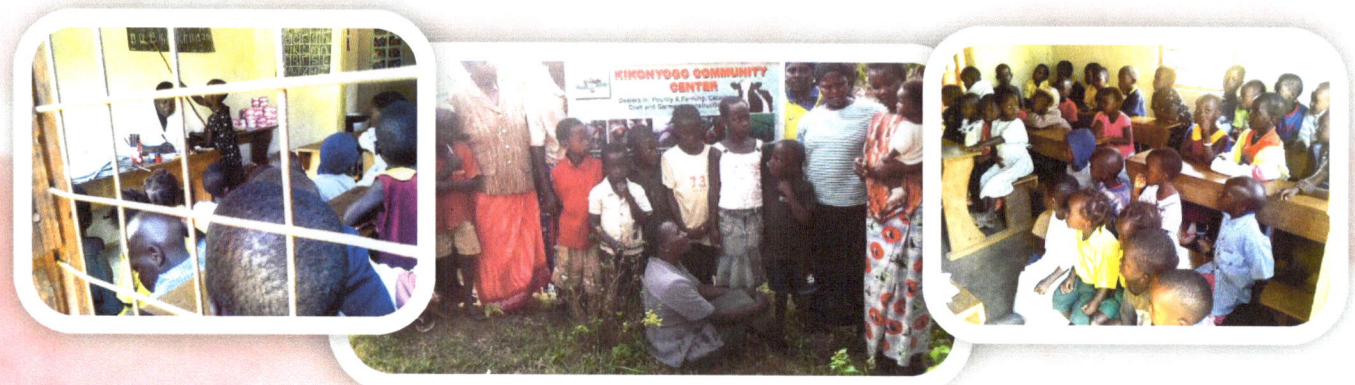

READ A BOOK Project

The READ A BOOK Project is run by the African Cultural Services Inc. (www.africaculture.org)

The major goal is to assist in building literacy levels as well as develop the reading and writing cultures in Uganda. ACS plans to donate books under the "Read a Book Project" to kindergartens and primary schools in Uganda. Schools that can afford a little will be encouraged to buy at a good price so as to support the cause on local level.

Meanwhile ACS will also launch a "donate a book" campaign where people can buy these books for any children all over the World. The proceeds go toward Kikonyogo Community Development Center (www.kicccuga.com) in Uganda, which helps with educating the poor as well as supporting the women especially the widowed, single or child mothers, to start self supporting projects for a better life.

READ A BOOK Project books will be written in English. But we encourage translations to other languages.

These books are also designed to promote cultural awareness and acceptance as well as boost critical thinking abilities, and use relevant themes to teach children moral lessons which their parents might never get the chance to teach them.